A WORLD OF HOLIDAYS

Cinco de Mayo

A WORLD OF HOLIDAYS

Cinco de Mayo

Sarah Vázquez

RSVP

RAINTREE
STECK-VAUGHN
PUBLISHERS
A Steck-Vaughn Company

Austin, Texas

Published by Raintree Steck-Vaughn Publishers, an imprint of Steck-Vaughn Company

Library of Congress Cataloging-in-Publication Data

Vázquez, Sarah.
    Cinco de Mayo / by Sarah Vázquez.
        p.   cm. – (A world of holidays)
    Includes bibliographical references and index.
    Summary: Introduces the customs and the practices of this Mexican holiday. Mexican Americans observe this holiday in California, Arizona, New Mexico, and Texas.
    ISBN 0-8172-5562-1 (hardcover)
    1. Cinco de Mayo (Mexican holiday) — Juvenile literature.
2. Mexico — Social life and customs — Juvenile literature.
[1. Cinco de Mayo (Mexican holiday).   2. Mexico — Social life and customs.   3. Holidays.]   I. Title.   II. Series.
F1233.V36   1999
394.26972 — DC21   98-12788
                                          CIP   AC

Acknowledgments

Editors: Sabrina Crewe, Kathy DeVico
Design: Sabine Beaupré
Artwork: Ceci Graphics
Planned and produced by Discovery Books

For permission to reproduce copyright material, the authors and publishers gratefully acknowledge the following:

Front cover Lawrence Migdale
Title page Suzanne Murphy-Larronde/DDB Stock
Contents page Devendra Shrikhande
page 6 Myrleen Ferguson Cate/PhotoEdit **page 7** (top) Lawrence Migdale, (bottom) Stewart Aitchsion/DDB Stock **page 8** Robert Fried/DDB Stock **page 9** (top) Robin J. Dunitz/DDB Stock, (bottom) Leslye Borden/PhotoEdit **page 10** (top) Leslye Borden/PhotoEdit, (bottom) Peter Chartrand/DDB Stock **page 11** Jay W. Sharp/DDB Stock **page 12** Luis Castañeda/Image Bank **page 13** J. P. Courau/DDB Stock **page 14** Don Klumpp/Image Bank **page 15** Institute of Texan Cultures **page 16** Lawrence Migdale **page 17** (top and bottom) Jose Luis Hernandez Garcia

page 18 (top and bottom) Lawrence Migdale **page 19** Jonathan Nourok/PhotoEdit **page 20** Tom Prettyman/ PhotoEdit **page 21** (top) David Young-Wolff/PhotoEdit, (bottom) Suzanne Murphy-Larronde/DDB Stock **page 22** (top) Lawrence Migdale, (bottom) Gary Conner/PhotoEdit **page 23** David Young-Wolff/PhotoEdit **page 24** Lawrence Migdale **page 25** (top) Tony Freeman/PhotoEdit, (bottom) Lawrence Migdale **page 26** Lawrence Migdale **page 27** Jeff Greenberg/PhotoEdit **pages 28/29** Devendra Shrikhande

 Contents

Fiesta Time!

Music fills the air! Colorful fireworks make the dark skies come alive! It is Cinco de Mayo, which means May 5th. Cinco de Mayo is a very important date for Mexican and Mexican American people.

A NATIONAL HOLIDAY

Cinco de Mayo is a national holiday in Mexico. It was the day when the Mexican army won the Battle of Puebla in 1862. The festival is celebrated in Mexico with speeches and parades. In Mexico, festivals are called "fiestas."

AN AMERICAN CELEBRATION

Mexicans in the United States celebrate Cinco de Mayo differently. They remember the battle, but they celebrate Mexican

Few Mexican fiestas are complete without beautiful fireworks.

On Cinco de Mayo, Mexican Americans celebrate their culture. They get together with other Americans for lively and colorful parades.

traditions as well. The biggest fiestas are in the southwestern part of the United States. This area had been part of Mexico until only a few years before the Battle of Puebla. Many people were still loyal to Mexico. After the battle, they wanted to celebrate Mexico's victory.

Today millions of Mexican Americans live in Arizona, New Mexico, California, and Texas. Wherever there is a Mexican community, you can be sure to find a fiesta on Cinco de Mayo.

This girl is dressed in national colors for Cinco de Mayo. Her red, green, and white clothes are the colors of the Mexican flag.

The People of Mexico

Mexico is one of the three countries that, with the United States and Canada, forms North America. It is a big and beautiful country with a special mixture of cultures.

NATIVE MEXICANS

The first people to live in Mexico were the Indians. The Olmec Indians settled in villages thousands of years ago. Later the Maya and other peoples built large cities. Millions of Indians lived in the cities and were ruled by kings. The Mayan community became a huge empire.

Hundreds of years later, another empire grew. The Aztec people built great cities. They were ruled by priests and warriors, and worshiped several gods. The Aztec empire conquered many other Mexican people and became the most powerful empire of all.

The Mayan Indians built beautiful cities and made huge sculptures from stone. You can see the ruins of some of these today.

The Aztec Indians wore splendid costumes at their festivals. These costumes are still worn at Cinco de Mayo.

This painting shows the Spanish conquering the Indians. They tried to destroy Indian culture and replace it with their own.

THE SPANISH CONQUEST

In 1519 soldiers arrived from Spain. They fought the Indians and conquered the Aztec empire. The Spanish ruled Mexico for three hundred years. They brought with them their language, their customs, and their Catholic religion.

Today many people in Mexico are mestizos. Mestizos are a mixture of Indian and Spanish. The Mexican culture that is celebrated on Cinco de Mayo is also a mixture of Indian and Spanish.

A Nation of Festivals

Masks are very traditional in Mexico. They are made and worn for many fiestas.

Mexico's long history has produced many days for Mexicans to remember. Almost every day there is a fiesta celebration in Mexico!

CELEBRATING HISTORY

Some of the religious celebrations are thousands of years old. Some are Christian holidays that came to Mexico with the Spanish people. Three thousand years of

The *charreria* is often a part of Mexican festivals. A *charreria* is similar to a rodeo. The *charros* (or cowboys) show their skills as horsemen. These *charros* are roping cattle.

Mexican history are remembered in dances, songs, and parades.

THE DAY OF THE DEAD

The Day of the Dead is a religious festival. It is a mixture of Aztec and Catholic beliefs. Mexicans believe that, on the nights of November 1st and November 2nd, the souls of people who have died come back to visit their families. Candlelight processions go to the cemeteries, where families celebrate with picnics and music.

Mexicans decorate their houses and public places for the Day of the Dead. Tables hold special toys and candies. Some are in the shape of skeletons and skulls!

SPECIAL DAYS

There are several holidays that celebrate special days in Mexican history. Independence Day on September 16th and Revolution Day on November 20th are very important holidays. Cinco de Mayo is also one of these special days.

❧ A Mexican Hero ❧

The story of Cinco de Mayo starts before the Battle of Puebla. It is the story of the people who struggled to make Mexico a free country.

Benito Juárez was a Zapotec Indian. In parts of Mexico, Zapotec and other Indian people still live much as they did in the time of Juárez.

BENITO JUÁREZ

In 1806 Benito Juárez was born in the village of San Pablo Guelatao. It was a poor mountain village, and there was no school. By the time Benito Juárez was eleven years old, his parents and grandparents had all died. When he was twelve, he left his village to go to school in the city of Oaxaca.

After many years of studying, Benito Juárez became a lawyer. In 1841 he became a judge.

Juárez was well known for being honest and standing up for the Indians. Because of this, the people of Oaxaca made him governor in 1847. In 1861 Juárez was elected president of Mexico.

A NEW PRESIDENT

It was a difficult time to be president. Mexico was no longer ruled by Spain. But there were still many fights in Mexico between the government and the leaders of the Catholic Church. Juárez was trying to take power away from the Church and the rich Spanish Mexicans. He wanted Indians and

Benito Juárez helped poor Indian people when he was a young lawyer. He went on to help many more when he became president of Mexico.

mestizos to have a say in ruling their country.

MEXICO IS INVADED

Another problem was that Mexico owed a lot of money to other countries, including France. When President Juárez refused to pay, France decided to invade Mexico. In December 1861, the French army attacked the port of Veracruz.

The Battle of Puebla

The French army defeated the people of Veracruz. In 1862 they started marching toward Mexico City.

THE TOWN OF PUEBLA

On May 4th, the French soldiers approached the town of Puebla. They made a camp for the night outside the town. The French army thought it would be easy for them to take over Puebla.

However, the Mexicans had different plans. President Juárez knew that the French army would soon arrive at Puebla. He told General Ignacio Zaragoza to try and defend the town. So General Zaragoza placed his soldiers in the hills outside of Puebla.

THE BATTLE BEGINS

On May 5th, the French soldiers attacked the Mexicans. To their surprise, the Mexicans fought hard.

This is a statue of General Zaragoza. He led the Mexican army to victory in the Battle of Puebla.

As it began to rain, the hills became muddy. It was hard for the French to keep up the battle. After a few hours, they were running out of bullets. They decided to give up. The Mexicans had won the Battle of Puebla!

AFTER THE BATTLE

There were more years of fighting after the Battle of Puebla. The French captured Mexico again and sent the emperor Maximilian to rule. But in 1867, Juárez led the Mexican people to victory against the French. At last, Mexico was free.

The French soldiers were well trained and had good weapons. They arrived with thousands of guns and many cannons. Many of the men in Zaragoza's army were not trained soldiers. They had poor weapons, and some carried only their work tools.

❧ Viva Mexico! ❧

President Juárez made Cinco de Mayo a national holiday. Today people still remember the battle and the brave people who fought for their country.

Men dressed as soldiers carry guns and farming tools in the Cinco de Mayo parade.

STAGING THE BATTLE

Sometimes Mexicans and Mexican Americans celebrate Cinco de Mayo by staging the famous Battle of Puebla. Men divide into two "armies" and dress up as Mexican and French soldiers. The make-believe battles help people to understand why they are celebrating.

The Fort of Loreto was an important place in the Battle of Puebla. From here, the Mexican army defended Puebla against the French.

THE BATTLE SITE

The town of Puebla has now grown into a big city. But you can still see where the Battle of Puebla took place. On the hills outside of Puebla are two forts. These forts were used by the Mexican army to defend the town. The Fort of Guadalupe is a ruin, but the Fort of Loreto is still standing.

THE WAR MUSEUM

In the Fort of Loreto, there is a museum. Visitors to the museum can see a model of the battle, set up to show what happened on Cinco de Mayo. There are weapons, uniforms, and other things to do with the Battle of Puebla. The museum also has many paintings of the battle.

This soldier's uniform is on display at the museum in the Fort of Loreto. You can also see a sword and binoculars that were used in the Battle of Puebla.

Colorful Costumes

Dressing up for Cinco de Mayo is great fun! There are many beautiful costumes to choose from.

COSTUMES FROM THE PAST

Some people wear Indian costumes for dancing or in parades. Different Indian peoples have their own traditional ways of dressing. Feathered headdresses and painted masks have been worn by some Indians for many hundreds of years.

Sombreros are the traditional hats worn by Mexican men.

These dancers have made wonderful headdresses to wear for the fiesta.

The sequins of the *china poblana* glitter and flash when women dance. Men wear the *charro* costume, and sometimes a serape.

Mexicans are famous for their wonderful woven cloth. Shawls and serapes woven in bright colors are worn every day as well as at fiestas. Serapes are blankets that men wear over one shoulder. When it gets cold, they can wrap their serapes around themselves.

NATIONAL DRESS

The *china poblana* dress was first worn in the state of Puebla. The skirt is completely covered with brightly colored sequins. The blouse of the dress is embroidered with silk threads or glass beads. Women usually wear a sash and shoes in the national colors. Their hair is decorated with bows.

The men's national costume is called the *charro*. This is also the name for a Mexican cowboy. The men wear a short jacket, tight pants, and riding boots. The outfit is decorated with embroidery and silver buttons.

The Music of Mexico

Music is very important in Mexico. In earlier times, the Indians believed that music kept the world moving. Today Mexicans and Mexican Americans still love music.

Musicians play traditional Indian music at Cinco de Mayo. This musician is blowing a conch shell.

THE FIRST MEXICAN MUSIC

Music has always played a part in all Mexican celebrations. The first Mexican people made instruments from bone, wood, and clay. They had drums, whistles, rattles, and instruments made from shells.

When the Spanish conquerors arrived in Mexico, they brought new kinds of music with them. They came with guitars, violins, and metal trumpets. As time went by, Indians started to play the new instruments. Eventually, they combined them with their own.

MARIACHI BANDS

On Cinco de Mayo, most of the music is played by mariachi bands. The bands can have from three to more than twenty members. They usually include violinists, guitarists, and trumpeters. There are often musicians playing the harp and the string bass as well. The mariachis play and sing songs that have been performed for hundreds of years.

The bands play some soft ballads, but they also play fast and happy tunes. The mariachis mostly play a type of music called the *son*. The *son* is a mixture of folk music from Spain, Mexico, and Africa. This type of music is not just to be played and sung. It is music everyone can dance to!

Some Mexican folk songs are hundreds of years old.

Cinco de Mayo is a time for mariachi bands to play for large crowds of people.

Dances in Mexico are part of a very old tradition. The Indians once danced for their gods. Today people dance at Cinco de Mayo simply to enjoy themselves!

At Cinco de Mayo, Mexican American children perform traditional dances in their schools.

Indians danced in large groups as part of their religion. They hoped their dances would bring them rain for their crops and victory in war.

DANCING KINGS

In the ancient cultures of Mexico, everyone danced, including priests and kings. The people danced to bring themselves good luck in hunting, wars, and harvests. Children were taught to dance and sing in special schools.

Later in Mexico's history, the Indian dances mixed with those of their Spanish invaders. Soon there were new dances, just as there was a new kind of music.

THE MEXICAN HAT DANCE

One of Mexico's famous dances is often called the Mexican hat dance. This has become Mexico's national folk dance. The dancers dance around a hat placed on the ground. They stamp their heels into the ground in fast steps. The pounding of their feet combines with the sound of the musical instruments.

It is very exciting to watch Mexican dancers as they go faster and faster.

23

Parades and Parties

In the United States, Cinco de Mayo is the largest Mexican American festival of the year. The fiesta usually starts with a great parade.

FLOATS AND FLOWERS

In many towns, the streets and trees are decorated with flowers, ribbons, and balloons. *Charros* on horseback, people carrying flags, and children in national dress parade down the street. Beautiful floats carry people in costumes. Mariachi bands play, and Indians perform dances.

After the parade, other festivities start. In Los Angeles, Cinco de Mayo festivities go on for three days. A big party takes place on Olvera Street, the oldest street in the city. There are hundreds of stands selling Mexican foods and crafts. The music and dancing continues into the evening.

A float covered in thousands of paper flowers is part of the fiesta parade.

Mexican crafts are everywhere at Cinco de Mayo. Painted puppets and straw hats are on sale at this stand.

FUN FOR CHILDREN

There is plenty for children to do at Cinco de Mayo. They can enjoy carnival rides, puppet shows, and games. A favorite with all children is the piñata. A piñata is made of papier-mâché and hung from a tree. Blindfolded children try to break it open with a stick. When the piñata breaks, enough candy for everyone comes tumbling out!

At picnics, children take turns hitting the piñata.

Food for the Fiesta

Traditional Mexican food includes dishes from all its cultures. Many delicious things to eat can be found at Cinco de Mayo!

FRESH FOODS

For fiestas, people like to prepare food that comes from their own area. At fiestas near the coast, there is plenty of fish and other seafood. In tropical areas, Mexicans use the fruit they grow, such as pineapples and mangoes. In all Mexican communities, you will find dishes made with beans, chilies, and corn.

The crowds wander around the stands at Cinco de Mayo. They can choose meals and snacks from hundreds of different stands.

Tortillas are still made in the traditional way. The cornmeal dough is rolled in the shape of a circle before it is cooked on top of a stove.

CORN AND TORTILLAS

Corn has been used in cooking for thousands of years. Indians once believed corn was sacred. They had special ceremonies for their corn gods.

Today many Mexicans still use corn every day. Tortillas made from ground corn are the most important Mexican food. Tortillas are used to make a huge number of dishes. They can be filled or topped with meat, cheese, beans, and salad. Tortillas are fried or baked to make tacos, enchiladas, and other dishes.

Let's Celebrate!

Join in the fun! Try making some Mexican cookies, and a small lantern to light at fiesta time.

MAKING POLVORONES

ASK AN ADULT TO HELP YOU.

Things you will need:
- a greased cookie sheet
- a large bowl
- a wooden spoon
- $1/2$ cup softened butter
- 4 tablespoons confectioners' sugar
- 1 teaspoon vanilla extract
- 1 cup all-purpose sifted flour
- 1 cup ground pecans
- water
- confectioners' sugar for rolling

Directions:
1. Preheat oven to 300 degrees.
2. Beat the butter and sugar together in a large bowl.
3. Add vanilla, flour, and ground pecans. Add a little water if the mixture is too dry.
4. Roll into about 20 small balls, and place balls on cookie sheets.
5. Bake for 30 to 40 minutes.
6. Remove from cookie sheets, cool, and roll in confectioners' sugar.

MAKING A FAROLITO

Materials:
- a paper lunch bag
- a pencil
- scissors
- a small flashlight
- glitter and sequins
- glue
- sand

Directions:
1. Draw any pattern or shapes you like on the paper bag.
2. Cut slits and holes in your patterns to make shapes for the light to shine through.
3. Decorate your bag with glitter, following the shapes you have drawn. You can stick on some sequins for more decoration.
4. Place some sand inside the bag, enough to make it stay open.
5. Put your flashlight inside the bag, setting it upright in the sand. Now watch your lantern glow!

Glossary

Celebrate To show that a certain day or event is special.

Charreria A show similar to a rodeo, where *charros* show their skills at riding horses and roping cattle.

Charro A Mexican cowboy.

China poblana A traditional Mexican dress with a skirt covered in sequins.

Community A group of people who live and work together.

Culture The customs, arts, and beliefs of a group of people at a certain time.

Custom A way of doing something that follows tradition.

Empire An area or country ruled by an emperor.

Enchilada A filled tortilla rolled, covered with chili sauce, and then baked.

Loyal Faithful to a person, group, or country.

Mestizos People who are part Spanish and part Indian.

National To do with a particular country and the people who live there.

Papier-mâché Paper that is soaked in glue. Before it dries and hardens, it can be molded.

Tradition A very old way of living that parents teach to their children.

Further Reading

De Varona, Frank. *Benito Juárez: President of Mexico.* Millbrook Press, 1993.

Gleiter, Jan. *Benito Juárez.* Raintree Steck-Vaughn, 1990.

MacMillan, Dianne. *Mexican Independence Day and Cinco de Mayo.* Enslow, 1997.

Palacios, Argentina. *Viva Mexico! A Story of Benito Juárez and Cinco de Mayo.* Raintree Steck-Vaughn, 1993.

Riehecky, Janet. *Cinco de Mayo.* Children's Press, 1994.

Index